Smoldering Hope

Hilary Pekoc

BookLeaf
Publishing

Presentation by *BookLeaf Publishing*

Web: www.bookleafpub.com

E-mail: info@bookleafpub.com

ISBN: 9789357440929

First edition 2023

DEDICATION

To my amazing children, Eddie and Faye. We are in this together.

ACKNOWLEDGEMENT

This book would not exist if not for magic and mystery with Thea, novels from Koenig, quiet love from Barb, reminders from Jeff that my story could save someone, and endless inspiration from Eddie and Faye.

PREFACE

This might make sense, or it may not. In my mind there is a well of songs, rich and muddy and mixed together from every person I've ever met, every peal of laughter and cry of heartbreak I've heard, every sunset I've ever seen. They fight with one another. Each one tries to shout the loudest, to be heard. Sometimes they just come pouring out of my mouth, and I want to run away and hide. Other times, I sing them proudly for all to hear, but no one is listening. So I write them down, hoping that when no one can hear my voice, someone might read my heart.

I considered ordering the poems from most despairing to more hopeful in my book, but ultimately chose to mix them together, because it reflects more accurately what real life is like. We do not suffer once, then fix it and feel better. We can--and often do--experience crushing defeat and encouraging support on the same day, then feel them over and over again. I have lived through violent pain and heartbreak, holding onto the hope that my life can become whatever I wish it to be. That determination sustained me through the worst times, when I thought I was lost. Beacons of hope are not a reward at the end of the suffering, but the support we need along the way.

Contradiction

days before,
alone was the safety--
closed and hidden, unseen.

now changed, unexpected,
forbidden, ejected,
and left all alone to dream.

hope unanswered,
stray bubbles of longing,
tears fall unchecked in the night.

cut loose, but unable
to escape and be stable.
free, but tethered down tight.

Kierkegaard

that single moment
a split-second decision
Life and Death

existence hanging on chance
a thread of longing
Life and Death

one idea to cling to--
truth is overrated.
whose truth is it anyway?

one person's truth
is another's dark lies.
Life and Death

who will choose?
truth is life.
Life and Death

is there a difference?
is there a choice?
Life and Death

we all just need
a place
to look at.

Secrets

unspoken thoughts
behind walls of blue,
hidden from all the world--
not safe from you.

these cracks in the shield
are so hard to seal,
please don't expose them--
just tell me it's real.

hollow dark words
in icy bare halls;
the color changes–
the dwindling guard falls.

why try to hide
what you already see?
no way to conceal
the devastation in me.

Park Swings

flying
nothing matters,
except...

the falling leaves
the rainbow in the sun
the tears that never fell
the smile.

soaring
everything matters,
except...

the pain of long ago
the words you didn't say
the storms you couldn't fight
yesterday.

striving
for only one thing--
to go higher.

Forget

one was never loved enough--
a soul untouched by heat.
tells the world that she is tough;
goes walking in the street.

one too scared to show her face,
broken by the sun.
wanders in search of a shaded place
where memories might be undone.

one all in white, fresh tears in her eyes,
with one she can't love at her side.
the setting is perfect, with lovely blue skies,
but pain is what "perfect" can't hide.

the three are so different, but so much the same,
all crying and praying for truth.
two on the down side of losing their smiles,
and one barely living her youth.

White Noise

moments of pleasure,
hours of warmth,
carefree fun,
no time to cry.

busy with laughter,
smothered by smiles.
happiness blacks out
the sadness pressing in.

constant enjoyment
suppressing the pain.
there must be a reason
it can't be like this.

trapped sounds,
bouncing endlessly,
reflecting quietly,
screaming for notice.

things unspoken,
but written about--
denied their right
to be heard.

the laughter is fading.
how long can it last?
honest silence,
as ever, deterred.

Muted

there aren't enough words
for the tears that I've cried;
I've scribbled in sobbing,
but something has died.

there aren't enough words
to display all this pain.
I'm empty, alone,
left to freeze in the rain.

there aren't any clouds
in the salt-laden skies.
face burnt from the sun
left to torture my eyes.

I'm too quick to forgive,
too nice to be mad.
so the guilt, chased by anger,
abandons me, sad.

I miss the close glances
and touches of light.
there aren't enough words
to protect me tonight.

Starlight Floating

the unexpected
will haunt your dreams
blur your thoughts
send you spinning.

this new perspective,
a shinier calm,
to open your eyes
to another world.

starlight floating,
impossible but true.
you never thought

a world so high
would be right at your feet.

Do You Know Me?

there's a tear in the box
where she keeps all her secrets.
it glistens a little,
but mostly it weeps.

she has all the words,
but can't find the actions
that would keep her from crying
alone when she sleeps.

they say fake it or make it,
so she smiles on in silence,
but she feels like a liar.
it doesn't ring real.

if you've stayed with her this far,
then maybe you're ready
to look into her eyes,
and ask, "what do you feel?"

Empty Cell

trying to talk, to sort out the thoughts,
but these bare walls throw everything back.

I've been lying on this ceiling so long,
I can't remember which way is up.

somewhere I know there's a child on a shore.
she'll find my bottle full of prayers, all my dreams.

no paper, no glass, just a whispered Song
that I sent out to float on the wind.

walls closing in, and everything's dark.
words breaking out, getting lost.

no one will hear. no north star. no direction to run from.
the minutes are passing. no place to go.

the stars! they're falling, dragging down my words.
I can't reach the sky.

Wax

empty heart,
empty head.
no one knows
until they're dead.

their cold touch
will never feel.
perfect people
are not real.

hopeless prayers,
useless words.
the only truth
is one that hurts.

colored feelings,
tears that burn.
there are some things
you never learn.

Teardrop Smile

I know in every teardrop
is the tiniest spark
of a smile.

and deep inside that little light,
the prism gathers
all the colors of the world.

the rainbow leads far
and away,
to a pool of gold

that is
the end
of tears.

Just

pillars crumble.
rocks can break.
what is there
time can't unmake?

raindrops fizzle.
soil dries.
who exists
and never cries?

once I sat
up in a tree,
thinking I was strong
and free,

forgetting trees
can die or burn;
forgetting leaves
are meant to turn.

never settle.
dare to scheme.
where is life
without your dream?

trust the moment.
let it be.
where am I
inside of me?

Melting

time is degrading
change is inevitable

your spirit is melting
the sickness is spreading

your sense of humor
is a puddle of liquid

lost

and you can't find the place
where it's solid again

your smile has faded
and it only makes you angry
when they try to find it

you never knew
it would end up like this

liquid
is all that's left.

Blurred

watercolors
dissolving,
never ending.

trees
green,
blue sky fading.

hate melting in love.

run. RUN!
be afraid.
you're sinking.

liquid feet,
horizon descending.

denied.
hidden.
deprived of the ending.

reach for color,
capture light.

mixing, intangible,
undefined
life.

Unwanted

cold,
alone.
telling myself not to cry,
to hurt.
force me to keep it inside.

the tears make me angry,
quiet overtakes me.
love is recast selfish need.

your pain makes me sorry.
your love overpowers me--
a hunger that no one can feed.

scared.
alone.
wishing for comfort from you--
a kiss,
without knowing it's hidden from view.

the darkness is empty.
my broken heart keening.
my thoughts won't allow me to sleep.

I stare but I don't see.
you want what I won't be.
my wounds are a secret I keep.

Chance Encounters

strangers,
connected for a moment
by some thought, a mutual curiosity.

the fleeting glimpse of a smile.
a large hand reaching out
for that tiny, cautious one.

and there is trust,
born somehow in that space in time,
seen behind the kindness of eyes and smile.

locked forever in that moment,
still warming the stage around it,
a smile hangs in the air.

Think

memory struggles,
stacked to the sky.
everyone's troubles
passing me by.

fanatical notions
pushed into my mind.
lifelong devotions
are so hard to find.

flying or falling,
I can't get to sleep.
the fishes are calling,
but the water's too deep.

trees on the ceiling,
a room filled with stone.
charged with no feeling,
I'm building my own.

hope, don't betray me;
there's too much to do.
they all say I'm crazy,
so maybe it's true.

Corner

how did I get here?
huddled in a burning house,
afraid but it's not what you think.

I built it.
set it on fire
'cause I couldn't feel the sun on my face.

in the rain,
I was happy.
I could taste the intensity.

all I wanted was more.
the downpour stopped.
the stickiness pressed in.

it choked me,
but I needed it,
so I stayed. I stayed...

on fire inside, smoldering,
and slowly

burning

out.

Full Circle

patterns,
jumped-on blocks of color.
buttons for friendship,
circles of truth.

the seasons,
up and down,
spiraling
eternity.

unbreakable
repeated dreams.
the clean sunrise.
yesterday, tomorrow.

again,
from good to bad,
small to great,
dust to dust.

the beginning or the end.
little details,
puddles to sand,
circling.

down
this spinning sphere,
and back
to me again.

Fall Down

kiss the gravel.
find your feet.
you bumped your head on the sky
and your chin on the ground.

brush off the grass stains,
climb up the air.
maybe the dirt
hit you that time.

get up. go on.
you are not the affliction.
the mountain is still there.
you're not beaten yet.

try again. go on.
this wasn't the first time,
and the future's uncertain,
but it won't be the last.

emerge. go on.
the memory hurts,
but it's nurturing new growth
and the sunrise is warm.

pour it out. go on.
the past is established.
the beginning is over.
it can't be made new.

reach up. go on.
leave your blood on the ground.
make a new ending.
write it down. live it here.